This book is dedicated to my amazing three children,
Miles, Hayden, and Dorothy. The true inspiration of
this series is watching the magic in their eyes when
we've cooked something delicious together. I hope
Tyler and Tofu encourage you to share the magic of
cooking with your children. —tf

To Daniele and Drew and our spirited whippets,
Tenacity and Penelope —cf

When cooking, it is important to keep safety in mind. Children should always ask permission
from an adult before cooking and should be supervised by an adult in the kitchen at all times.
The publisher and author disclaim any liability from any injury that might result from the use,
proper or improper, of the recipes contained in this book.

Library of Congress Cataloging-in-Publication Data is available.
ISBN 978-0-06-204760-1 (trade bdg.) — ISBN 978-0-06-204761-8 (lib. bdg.)

The artist created the illustrations with pen and ink and colored them digitally.
Typography by Craig Frazier
14 15 16 17 18   SCP   10 9 8 7 6 5 4 3 2 1
    ❖
First Edition

Tyler

MAKES A BIRTHDAY CAKE!

WRITTEN BY
Tyler Florence

ILLUSTRATED BY
Craig Frazier

HARPER
An Imprint of HarperCollinsPublishers

"Tofu, I forgot today's your birthday!" shouted Tyler. "Don't worry, I'm going to throw you a party that you will never forget and make you the biggest, best cake ever. Wait a minute...

"I don't know how to make a cake. Let's go to the bakery and find out how."

"Hi, Mr. Baker," Tyler said. "I'm having a birthday party today, and your carrot cake is my absolute favorite!"

"Just in time, Tyler," Mr. Baker said. "I'm actually making a fresh one in the back. Do you want to come help me?"

"Yes!" said Tyler.

"This is my kitchen," said Mr. Baker. "This is where all of the amazing cakes you see out front are made. We can create anything you set your imagination to."

"What about a spaceship birthday cake? Or a race-car birthday cake? Can you even make a pirate-ship birthday cake?"

"Yes, I can, Tyler!"

"Tyler," Mr. Baker asked, "have you ever made a cake before?"

"I make pancakes all the time with my mom and dad. Does that count?" asked Tyler.

"Of course! So you'll certainly recognize the ingredients I have on the table."

"I sure do," Tyler said. "Flour, buttermilk, eggs, and butter. Pineapple and a whole lot of carrots! Where did you get so many?"

"Well, Tyler, just imagine..."

"...we're on a farm with lots and lots of fresh, yummy carrots."

"But I don't see them anywhere."

"That's because they grow underground," said Mr. Baker.

"My mom puts carrots in my lunch box all the time because she says they're good for my eyes."

"That's right, Tyler. They're packed with vitamin A, which helps you see better," said Mr. Baker.

"What else do we need?"

"The next thing we need is raisins."

"Raisins come from grapes. Right, Mr. Baker?"

"Right, Tyler. As these juicy grapes dry out in this beautiful California sunshine they become chewy, sweet raisins. Those are going to taste delicious in our cake."

"Mmmm. What's next?"

"We're going to the orchard.
Hold the ladder steady,
Tyler," Mr. Baker shouted.

"What are you doing up in
that tree?" asked Tyler.

"I'm picking fresh walnuts. Underneath these skins there is a hard shell, and inside that is the nut. Walnuts can be such a tasty addition to cake."

"What else do we need?"

"Aloha, Tyler."

"Whoa! Where are we now?" Tyler asked.

"Hawaii! It's where I get pineapples. They have a tart flavor that blends well with all of the other ingredients. Pineapples got their name because they look like big pinecones."

"Is that it?" Tyler asked.

"No! There are two more very special ingredients. We add these to the cake for flavor and a terrific smell."

"I already smell something really good," Tyler said.

"That's cinnamon," said Mr. Baker. "It's the bark of these trees."

"What's that other sweet smell?"

"That's vanilla. Did you know it comes from these beans? You can't make carrot cake without cinnamon and vanilla."

"Cool! What else do we need?"

"We'll need milk to make the main
ingredient for our frosting—cream cheese."

"I know milk is used to make cheese, but cream cheese on a cake? I usually put that on my bagels," said Tyler.

"I like it on my bagels, too, but if we add some sugar, it becomes a sweet, silky cake frosting that looks like snow!"

In the kitchen, Tyler and Mr. Baker shred the carrots and chop up the walnuts. They measure the dry ingredients in one bowl and the liquid ingredients in another. Then they combine the two and fold in the carrots, pineapple, and walnuts.

They pour the cake into a pan
and stick it into the oven.

While it's baking, they mix up
some frosting.

After the cake cools, they begin to ice it.

"Tyler, is this your birthday cake?" asked Mr. Baker.

"No…it's for my dog, Tofu. It's his birthday today."

"It's a good thing I checked!" said Mr. Baker. "Tofu shouldn't eat this kind of cake. It's too rich for dogs."

"Oh no!" exclaimed Tyler. "I promised to make Tofu the best birthday ever. But without a cake, we can't have a party. Now what do I do?"

"Hmm," said Mr. Baker. "While you set up the party, I'll try to come up with something."

"Tofu, this is going to be the coolest party ever! Let's get the rest of the supplies for your birthday."

"What do we need? Party hats, check. Noisemakers, check. Face paint, check. Refreshments, check. Games, check. Balloons, check."

"It looks like I'm here right in time," said Mr. Baker. "I came up with a special recipe that's just for dogs. I'm sure you can tell which one's for Tofu!"

"Wow, you did it, Mr. Baker. These hounds can't wait to chow down!" said Tyler. "Who knew they were such party animals?"

"Happy birthday, Tofu!" said Tyler. "Don't forget to make a wish. Mine is that I can keep cooking with my best friend—you!"

TYLER'S CARROT CAKE
AND FROSTING RECIPE
{FOR HUMANS, NOT DOGS}

Recipe courtesy of Tyler Florence / *Dinner at My Place*
Yield: 1 large cake, serves 8–10
Time: 1 hour 45 minutes

Ingredients:

1½ cups finely minced carrots
½ cup crushed pineapple, drained
3/4 cup finely chopped walnuts (optional)
2½ cups all-purpose flour, plus extra for pan
1 teaspoon baking powder
1 teaspoon baking soda
¼ teaspoon ground allspice
½ teaspoon ground cinnamon
½ teaspoon freshly ground nutmeg
a pinch of kosher salt
1 cup buttermilk
¼ cup molasses
4 large eggs
3/4 cup vegetable oil
1½ cups dark brown sugar

Directions:

Preheat oven to 375 degrees F. Butter a jelly-roll pan and line with parchment. Set aside.

Combine carrots, pineapple, and walnuts in a medium bowl. Set aside. Mix together flour, baking powder, baking soda, spices, and salt in a large mixing bowl. Mix together buttermilk, molasses, eggs, oil, and dark brown sugar in a separate medium bowl.

Now add the buttermilk mixture to the flour mixture and stir with a wooden spoon to make the batter, then fold in the carrot mixture. Pour into the prepared pan and bake in the preheated oven for 25 to 30 minutes, until the cake is set and springs back when gently pressed in the middle. Remove the pan from the oven and allow the cake to cool on a rack while you prepare the Cream Cheese Frosting.

Once the cake has cooled, carefully remove the cake from the pan. Cut into three equal-size rectangles by cutting the cake lengthwise twice. Stack the cake up into three tiers with Cream Cheese Frosting in between each layer. Frost the outside of the entire finished cake, smoothing off the edges and corners (an offset spatula works well).

Cream Cheese Frosting:

2 pounds cream cheese, room temperature
2 sticks unsalted butter, room temperature
2 cups powdered sugar
1 teaspoon vanilla extract
1 teaspoon lemon zest

Using a standard mixer, combine cream cheese and butter in a large mixing bowl until it is blended and has a smooth, light texture. Add the powdered sugar, vanilla, and lemon zest and beat until combined. Continue to beat until smooth and glossy, about 7 minutes.

Ask and be safe. Make sure no one in your company is allergic to walnuts before you add them to your carrot cake!

Carrots are a root vegetable because the most commonly eaten part grows under the ground—although the greens are edible as well! They get their bright orange color from beta-carotene, which turns into vitamin A when eaten. Carrots can be eaten raw or cooked and are super healthy, providing a rich source of fiber, antioxidants, and minerals.

Pineapples get their name because they look like a pinecone. They are a fruit that is typically grown in tropical climates, including some islands. Under their tough skin is a juicy and sweet fruit that is usually eaten raw. Chunks of pineapple can be used in salads, desserts, ice cream, juices, and even on pizzas.

Did You Know?

Raisins are shriveled-up, sun-dried grapes. Purple grapes make dark raisins, and green grapes make light or golden raisins. They are supersweet and the perfect snack to eat by the handful. They are also a great addition to cookies and cakes because of their chewy texture and sweetness.

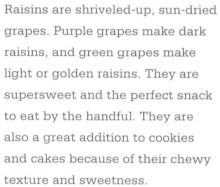

We call walnuts nuts but they are actually seeds. They come in a hard shell that is made of two halves. Walnuts are considered a "superfood" because they're loaded with protein, vitamins, minerals, and antioxidants. They are used a lot in baking and desserts because they add great crunch and taste. They are also a great snack food to eat raw by the handful! But some people are allergic to any kind of nut and can get really sick. *Before cooking or even eating them, be sure that you and no one in your company has a nut allergy.*

Cream cheese is soft and has a very mild taste. It is best known for being spread on bagels and crackers. It is just as delicious when you blend it with ingredients such as sour cream or yogurt to make dip for vegetables, chips, or crackers. Mixed with sugar, it makes the perfect cake frosting!

TYLER'S DOG CARROT CAKE RECIPE

{FOR DOGS, NOT HUMANS}

Feeds 2–3 dogs

Prep time: 20 minutes
Cook time: 45 minutes

Ingredients:
2 eggs
½ cup peanut butter
½ cup grape-seed oil
1 teaspoon vanilla extract
⅔ cup honey
2 cups shredded carrots
2 cups whole wheat flour
2 teaspoons baking soda

Directions:
Preheat oven to 325 degrees F.

In a mixer combine the eggs, peanut butter, oil, vanilla, honey, and carrots; blend well until batter is smooth. Sift together the flour and baking soda and fold the wet mixture into the dry mixture. Evenly coat a nonstick muffin tin with cooking spray and scoop mixture into ¾ of the volume of the cup.

Bake in the oven for 45 minutes. Let the cake cool in the pan for 10 minutes, then turn out cakes onto a cooling rack to cool completely.